Little Leo Monkey

Written by Suzanne Taylor

This book is dedicated to my two little monkeys, Izzy & Theo, and to my parents, Dorothy & Keith

1st Edition 2024

Text & Layout Copyright protected 2024

Little Leo Monkey

This book belongs to

Little

_____

Monkey

Little Leo Monkey

Little Leo Monkey,

Small and sweet.

Hairy hands,

Furry feet.

Never still,

Play he will.

Leaping, hopping.

Only stopping

For Mummy hugs

And a groom for bugs.

Juicy fruits,

Long green shoots.

Bright yellow sun,

Visitors come.

Hide and seek

With monkey friends.

Playing till the daylight ends.

Chatter, chatter, squeak!

Is how they speak.

Climbing trees,

Forest playground home.

Monkeys

Free to climb and roam.

Just the way

it's meant to be.

Monkeys were born

to be free!

Little Leo monkey,

Small and sweet.

Hairy hands,

Furry feet.

Never still,

Play he will.

Leaping, hopping,

Only stopping

For Mummy hugs

And a groom for bugs.

Juicy fruits,

Green green shoots.

Bright yellow sun,

Visitors come.

Hide and seek

With monkey friends.

Playing till the daylight ends.

Chatter, chatter, squeak!

Is how they speak.

Climbing trees,

Forest playground home.

Monkeys

Free to climb and roam.

Just the way it's meant to be.

Monkeys were born to be free!

MUNCHING MONKEYS

Old Mrs Macaque
Liked to snack
On fruit throughout the day.
Her favourite were plums
The juice tickled her gums
And made her chuckle away.

Old Mr Macaque
Ate apples for his snack.
He'd munch and crunch all day.
The juice was sticky and sweet.
It dripped on his feet
And kept creepy crawlies away.

Uncle Macaque
Liked nothing better than the CRACK
Of crunchy carrots between his teeth.
He'd sit by the tree stump, such a friendly chap,
And share with the rabbits beneath

Auntie Macaque
Had a favourite too
Sweet potato her choice of things to chew.
She loved them raw, mashed, chipped or in stew
However they were served
They would do!

Little Leo is a macaque monkey who lives in the forest surrounding Angkor Wat temple, in Cambodia, Southeast Asia.

Many monkey species are endangered, including Leo's.

One of the main threats they face is due to the illegal pet trade in small monkeys.

Baby monkeys are often stolen from their mothers and sold as pets.

Some people dress the monkeys in nappies and clothes, thinking it is adorable. They feed them sweets, cakes and other foods which make them ill.

Once the monkeys have grown and are no longer small and cute, they are abandoned back in the forest. They don't know how to behave like a wild monkey or how to make friends, nor do they know how to forage for food.

There are several conservation groups who are trying to put an end to the captivity of monkeys the whole world over.

While they are extremely cute, monkeys should never be kept as pets. They need to live in the wild with other monkeys where they will be happy.

Remember – monkeys were born to be free!

Photo Gallery

Credits and thanks for photography go to a number of people who kindly upload their amazing shots to Canva Pro.
Others are author's own photos taken during numerous visits to the Monkey Forest, Stoke.
I highly recommend a trip!

Eak8dda

Jayantibhai Movaliya

fontoknak   ittipon2002   Rakesh K   Michydev

Apricot Jam   sansara   ittipon2002   Fotosmurf03

OceanFishing

f4f

prerna jain

esmeraldaedenberg

TryMyBest

Fluky Fluky

rvimages

Mumemories

Lincoln Beddoe

Dopeyden

fontoknak

anon

Micheydev

fontoknak

Wirestock

John Crux

Ayden Stofen

fontoknak

056314d4_392

sytilin

MKC100

a_m_o_u_t_o_n

Fike2308

Look carefully at the pictures...
Can you find all the differences?

www.ingramcontent.com/pod-product-compliance
Lightning Source LLC
Chambersburg PA
CBHW042355070526
44585CB00028B/2941